Emné Nasereddine

THE
DANCE
OF THE
FIG TREE

Translated and introduced
by **Stuart Bell**

Published 2023 by the87press
The 87 Press LTD
87 Stonecot Hill
Sutton
Surrey
SM3 9HJ
www.the87press.co.uk

English translation © Stuart Bell, 2023
Translator's introduction © Stuart Bell, 2023
Cover image © Philippe Efe, 2023

First published as 'La danse du figuier' by Mémoire d'encrier
© Mémoire d'encrier, 1260 rue Bélanger, bur. 201, Montréal, Québec,
H2S 1H9. © Emné Nasereddine, 2021.

The moral right of x has been asserted in accordance with the
Copyright, Designs and Patents Act 1988

ISBN: 978-1-7393939-3-9

Printed and bound by CPI Group (UK) Ltd, Croydon, CR0 4YY
Design: Stanislava Stoilova [www.sdesign.graphics]

EMNÉ NASEREDDINE was born in France in 1990 and grew up in Lebanon where she studied French literature at the Saint Joseph University in Beirut. Her poetry explores her experiences of immigration, loss and mourning, the lives of Lebanese women, and the customs and traditions of southern Lebanon. *The Dance of the Fig Tree* is her first book and was awarded the 2021 Émile-Nelligan Prize. She lives in Montreal.

STUART BELL is an editor and translator of French literature. His previous publications include *Bird me* (2021), shortlisted for the 2022 Oxford-Weidenfeld Prize, and *Yo-yo Heart* (2022), selected by The Poetry Book Society as their 2022 Winter Translation Choice. He is currently editing the second volume of the87press South London Cultural Review, an essay collection entitled *On Feminist Films*, forthcoming in 2024.

This book was completed during a Translator in Residence stay at Cambridge University in the Lent term of 2023.

The translator would like to thank the staff and students of Corpus Christi College for their warmth and hospitality.

Translator's introduction

The Dance of the Fig Tree is Emné Nasereddine's first book of poetry. Originally published in 2021 by Mémoire d'encrier, it also won the Émile-Nelligan Prize that year for a collection by a writer under the age of thirty-five. Born in France, Emné studied French literature at the Saint Joseph University in Beirut and now lives in Montreal. The poems tell the story of moving between these disparate places, of the people and ties to the past, lost and then commemorated. They offer a deeply personal meditation on childhood, grief, exile and broken lineage. As the prologue explains, the eponymous fig tree no longer stands. This was a tree that once danced, under which she danced as a child. The poems written in its name resonate joy and pain, transcending time and now, in first-time translation, also language.

The collection is made up of three parts, each named after a woman the poet holds dear. The first is 'Téta', the grandmother, a Lebanese native who loses her children and homelife, a survivor of the horrors of occupation and war. Téta's voice bears witness to the plundering of the land, yet too channels the customs and traditions of her forebearers. She draws up her final will, leaving behind not material goods but the wisdom of ancestral ways and rites. Instead of bequeathing her legacy to her kin, she gifts season and myth to the infinite spirits of the Arabic world: Rabih, Majed, Zaher, Ali, Boutheina, Magida, Mona, Charifé, Fatima. Mythic in her own right, Téta is an all-seeing observer of the manmade: 'Beyond the mulberry tree it's hell, Téta tells me', and the natural: 'She sees something crossing / a wish fall apart / a pheasant fall asleep'. Seeing past her present moment, Téta fears for Emné's future domestic security, encouraging her to follow the traditions of the people: 'Téta does not want poetry / she wants to know when I plan on marrying / you cannot live alone / you need a man for the roof / children for old age'. More globally, Téta too anticipates Lebanon's wider undoing in collective memory, warning her successors: 'Do not forget the sea / do not forget the fig trees.' The poems of this collection are the guise of a reply.

The second section is entitled 'Fadwa', named after Emné's mother who has died. She is survived by the grief-stricken Téta, who looks to the stars to recover her lost daughter. Fadwa's absence is deeply felt throughout this section, from her rainy funeral rites to one starless night when Téta, distraught with loss, howls her name at the moon. We learn that Fadwa wore scarves and amber perfume. A theatre actress in life, she is remembered for her morning coffees, the unique shape of her nose when viewed in side profile, the beauty spot on her chin. After her passing, Emné laments: 'I am not allowed the jewellery / nor your red scarf and its snowy lacework / what do they know about love Mama?' The loss of her mother, and of the fig tree of home, ignite feelings of turmoil and injustice as she vows to Fadwa in death: 'I promise / upheaval / and triumph / for you and Téta'. If *The Dance of the Fig Tree* exists at all, it stems from a universal human need to find one's way home, and from the sanctity of a promise made from daughter to mother: 'I will talk about you / all will remember'.

Section three bears the name 'Emné'. The verses channel memories of a father disappeared, the discontent of exile, and the tensions within cultural and ethnic difference. Here she struggles to acclimatise to metallic Montreal where the 'winter-women' live and tomato plants fail. She takes recourse in memories of faraway pomegranate trees and in mental imprints of the skies, waters and birds of the Mediterranean. Recalling her lost family lineage brings suffering: 'I cough my memory / laugh mad cold / am I going to die tied to madness?

/ the real finds me / pale and slow'. This pain of loss and dislocation fuses with expectant, repeated urges to write: 'my hips / have been stripped of the lullabies / I wrote, narrated / then made rot / in the coffins of the north / all stories merge and still today / my child is not born'. At times sensual, ultimately optimistic, the poems in this final section bear the scars of war and a homesickness as political as it is personal.

If the fig tree is uncontested as the collection's central image, the sea too is a core emblem. Emné tells her mother to take a piece of it with her into the afterlife, and then, in her own private mourning ritual, paints her eyelids to match 'the colours of the sea'. Later, now far from home, she listens to the sound of the waters while crying and praying. She longs to return to the Lebanese city of Baalbek, recalling Proust's fictional seaside town 'Balbec' where the narrator of *In Search of Lost Time* spends summers with his mother and grandmother. Retracing the many unnatural breakages in her family tree, she echoes Proust's final volume *Time Regained* within the lines: 'the absurd regained / and time unspent'. Beyond the sea, the reimagined skies of Baalbek – also known as 'Heliopolis' in antiquity – and of Lebanon figure throughout. The sky is where Fadwa now dwells, having governed it in life, as we are told: 'I had a mother who used to lift the sky / with her two hands'.

Wind, rain and sun are natural forces to be withstood, yet remain the channelers of blissful sensory memory. Akin to Proust's child narrator, Fadwa too cries over wild flowers, yet here they take the form of native-Mediterranean anemones, or 'windflowers', known for their unsteadiness even in light breeze. Later, the sun warms her lingering ambergris scent, revelling in her perfume, as if she were still living. Fresh mornings stir the aroma of wild thyme. So prevalent are spices, they take on epic forms such as 'the sumac sun' and the recurring figure of the 'cardamom woman' who may or may not be a figment of the infantile imaginary. The collection closes with the image of the sun: 'I will not sunfade', a line inspired by a neologism in 'Separation Poem' by Quebec poet Gaston Miron: 'Il n'empêche / que par moments ton absence fait rage / qu'à travers cette absence je me désoleille'. ('Still / there are moments when your absence is enraging / and through this absence I sunfade'). In reclaiming this neologism, the poet embraces a form of non-standard French that she has long admired, born out of what she calls: 'the hostile climate in Canada', now transposed from one love poem to another.

In a 2021 interview, Emné speaks of the Covid-19 pandemic during which her grandmother fell ill and began losing her memory. This loss in process, she explains, is what first catalysed her writing, a longstanding need to bring her grandmother and her late mother 'face to face with their territory' in words. Speaking on television, Emné affirms much of what the poems tell us by detailing her grandmother's biography. Having married at the age of thirteen, she raised ten children. She worked in the tobacco fields and was a resistor during the Israeli occupation. As if channelling the life-force of this inspirational matriarch via the maternal-filial line, the poetic voice declares: 'I am the daughter of the daughter', a girl set in 'countryside ways'. Following her grandmother, the poet becomes a working woman who uses her hands: a stitcher of dreams. Yet, while the elder woman is duty-bound, the granddaughter finds freedom in writing. Such threads of generational similitude and difference run throughout the women's lives, as one poem laments: 'our hands busy / my hands shameful', yet insisting nevertheless: 'I betrayed no-one / neither the mountain / nor the pomegranate trees'. Memorably, in the final 'Fadwa' poem, the three generations of women are likened to Bertolt Brecht's 'Mutter Courage', heroine of the play *Mother Courage and Her Children* in which the maternal yet hardy Anna Fierling loses her three children against the backdrop of The Thirty Years War.

Emné explains during the interview that in the wake of her mother's death 'children were left out' of the mourning rituals. She tells of the present-day need to return in writing to the confusion and disbelief of that period: 'I remember my brother, my father, my uncles returning. I had stayed at home. I could not make sense of what had happened because I had been deprived of that moment.' It feels important to note that she never writes in her mother's voice; instead the 'I' roams freely within the surrealist memory of the event itself. The same is true of poems in the other named sections: it is never precisely Téta, Fadwa or Emné the individual who is speaking. The tree's dance conjures many voices, uniting people and moments in time, commemorating all and excluding none. Emné says that she hoped to find within poetry an answer to the question: 'What am I doing here in Montreal?' In reaching towards an answer, the poems take us back in time to Baalbek, to Nmairiyeh, and lay to rest the women so dearly loved in a place of togetherness and safety. And so too we readers are called upon to bear witness to it all through the welcoming invitation: 'Sit down all of you under the fig trees.'

Stuart Bell

For my grandmother Khawla and my sister Khawla

In memory of Fadwa

I love you
you who leave with the wind as your banner.

Nadia Tuéni

Prologue

In 2017 my mother died in Nmairiyeh, in southern Lebanon. Her funeral was a reflection of her life. A theatre of the absurd.

I laughed out loud before falling silent, beside my childless grandmother.

During this period I was reading *The Earth Stilled* by Nadia Tuéni. One of her poems was, for me, a source of anxiety. 'O gardener of my memory, plant a flower of certainty… Tell me which tree matches the ground where I am going to sit, when light and darkness join.' The fig tree under which we used to dance as children has been cut down. I no longer knew where to go. Inside a sadness that my body knew well, I ended up fleeing without leaving a trace.

In poetry I saw the possibility of living in a place and rediscovering the tenderness of the women who raised me. To write means to shelter them, like a maternal gesture.

I wrote in order to make a home. To stand overlooking all horizons. To anchor myself between sky and mother. With my grandmother who carries our memory. In the shadow of the fig tree that goes on dancing.

Emné Nasereddine

Téta

Here is how my story starts
Téta is brewing tea
from the foreign land that has settled itself
on the ground floor
of her house
      singing

my aunt carries the tray
with the cups
the tea pot
the sugar
then steps out into the street
to face the war

Téta is boiling oil in three large pans
her resistance secrets
she, guardian of the country
ready to welcome
the shadow rising over the doorstep

around her legs, too many children
with mixed-up names
silently awaiting
the maternal act

Beyond the mulberry tree it's hell, Téta tells me
I run smile
fast-footed

the sun has set
there will be cries on return
but I saw the other side
and there were no men dead

how to tell her that healing begins now?

She still thinks
that the claimants of the south
never left
the end of her street

beyond the mulberry tree
thugs were on the lookout for
the shape of her dreams

above her bed
yesterday's markings
      bullet-riddled wall
my finger excavates the hole

was anyone still standing?

Téta handpicks lentils like a king deciding who lives
later I sneak another peek
make a second judgement
on what her eyes could not see

or was it the mercy of those who were starving?

I watch her
her, perched, shrouded in silence
staring at the road with a thinking mouth
she sees
something crossing
a wish fall apart
a pheasant fall asleep

what do they think about, those who do not read poetry?

suddenly an itch in the palm of her hand
she tells me
soon I am going to harvest some money
inchallah Téta
the right hand is prosperity

My lover tells me about a chaotic dream
teeth falling out
I tell him the bad news
and suddenly my ramblings are funny

is he laughing at you Téta?
the jaws of death
ancestral knowledge
the crescent moon
the pillar of instincts

is he blind to the language of the night?

I write about you
your woman's nights
the mysteries of Turkish coffee
a roof handed over to the enemy
your rebellious heart

can you hand me another secret?

Téta does not want poetry
she wants to know when I plan on marrying
    you cannot live alone
    you need a man for the roof
    children for old age

her stomach is miscarriage heavy
her back arching over tobacco leaves
abandoned by all God's hopes

today she still cries over
the one who made her a woman at thirteen
tears of love
tenderness
skin dream and naked face

mother already virginal

today she still cries
like we cry for her father

My grandfather said no several times
when they invited him into paradise
he could not name
his wife's silence
the scar on her forehead
the carvings in her house
and this bitter taste left behind by men
playing misery games
thought up on the roadside
no
no, he insisted
like revenge for a lousy life
this was all he could say and juggle with the soil

Téta
you put the tools in my hand
and I must learn to build
the second storey of your house
in the second following the war
under the clouds that only you see

I breastfeed the stone, I prepare the foundations
and suddenly notice that the children have already left
I daren't tell you
I'd rather cement empty ground

You bring your forgotten children to the sea
your hand dances
and the sumac calls out
from the edge of the abyss
your hand smiles
and the tobacco leaves stir
the groaning of the orange trees
your eyes squinting in the sunlight
and the smell of the Mediterranean

Téta answers bitterly
will we see one another again someday
and together love the face of God?
do not leave, my children
there will be so little life to live
do not forget the sea
do not forget the fig trees

who will carry my tiredness?

Téta declares her final will
Rabih, springtime
hyacinth of my sleep
to you I leave the sea
that has aided you so
you will cross it as do
handsome men of war
you will forget to return to me yet you will remain
my favourite
Rabih, prodigal child
light of the Mediterranean
hear me
hear me

My son is already gone
    a bullet burrowed in his shoulder

Majed, glorious one
you will have time as companion
you will avenge me with words
yours shall be noble
that will speak of the love of Wissale
Majed, magnificent one
take the bees too
but do not tell anyone

Look how I love you
me, Em Majed, stripped of my name
mother only through you

my son has forgotten the memory of the verb

Zaher, the loner, to you I give my malice
my acts of perseverance
the armour of wit
Zaher the trickster
too loutish
here are the orange trees
do not cut them
they will save you, one day

Stand up straight, stop running
my son flees the length of his shadow
not realising he has conquered the night

Ali, the neglected, the middle child
to you I leave the wind, where you have roamed
since your childhood
and the innocence of the body
your name stands with the friends of God
Ali, in the heavens
Ali, so high
take care not to disappear

My son is a golden canary
I made him a nest beside mine
yet he prefers the Syrian wind

the sky there may be more beautiful

Boutheina, devoted one
to you I leave my tears
the humus of sadness
and some fistfuls of soil
to help you survive
Boutheina smile
before Mohamad
a poet spoke of you
love in madness
flood of memory

My daughter cries for the windflowers, the blackcurrants
and calvaries the world over
it is time to feed laughter

despite Lebanon

Magida
to you I leave my face
a stony voice
and welcoming arms just when
no-one expects it
Magida conqueror
you will wear the robes of patience
in your lemon tree garden
take all my desires
learn to say I love you

Hold my legs, flee with me
have we birthed too many children?
do we love them rightly enough?
my daughter, if only we left this place
perhaps we would be gentle mothers

Mona, stealthy panther
I name you resilience
she who wishes and gives her voice in return
Mona, goddess of all wishes
you will have clarity to banish madness
forced exile that will save childhood
and a body pervious to the twisting world

My daughter can name the clouds
and pray the nameless language
body rejoicing
return at long last
    dug-out backwash
to our ever star-filled sky

Charifé, miraculous one
I have shown you my weakness and from it flowed
one who never bowed
before ugliness
who never
shuddered
at the sound of thunder
Charifé mane scorpion
show me the courage to face
what lies before me

My daughter loves land men olive trees
justice thief
give me, gift me
muscle for thought

Fatima, weaner of heavens and land
the dawn is written on your face
take motherhoods
and the fluttering of butterflies
Fatima, devotion
to you I leave the bed in which I slept
at thirteen
my elder one
return to my breast

My daughter gets up before sunrise
breaks her bread
feeds the children
and your bit, my beloved?

Fadwa, to you I leave love and beauty
lukewarm with tiredness, like you
life will sever the roots
from your hips
difficult children
the far-away man
water bubbles in the lung's hollow
Fadwa, sacrificed one
you are the woman of the tale
you will be in the poems
and in the cradles of the theatre

Play, turn, show me your artful heels
one last time

my daughter has slid underground
the theatre is dead, not even the stage remains

Fadwa

Where does childhood end?
Where does vastness begin?
I saw the dead body
time stops here
the child sees and suddenly its skin has aged
many centuries
the child sees and asks
what do we do with the body?
like a killer who already knows
that the body is a bother
that the body must be hidden

And then what?
I ready my wedding clothes
unsure of the sun
of the day to follow
like the riddle of childhood
     without you Mama, what can come of the world?
here is where chance comes in
here is where God steps in

Rest day
there was sunshine two children and their laughter
that I tasted
not a drop of wind that day pebbles
sand   Fadwa
water   mother
clay   your name
mud then cement
emptiness filled
earth returned to earth
the hollow dust
the body inside
light of my eyes
towards which abyss?
take a piece of sea with you
the heavens will gift it to you
in the hole
she is lifeless
amidst
fertile substance   wormy compost
sense of touch gone
panic pit
the world
    and its strangeness
the cavity
a cube
a thing
in the pockets of my memories, mama is dancing
I smile at her

Rain the day after
is falling and watching
the burial of the one carried away
the perpendicular body in the openings to paradise
three generations come to greet you
bodies awkward
from breakages

    nobody teaches us how to leave childhood behind

nightfall, gathered cousins
mimic your gestures
never-ending the map
of the sky your voice
we are at the theatre of the dead
we are playing your part and our laughter shapes
the original prayer

it is the offering made to the living

but the night is suddenly
over

You left the day after Ashura
prayers are abundant
and your name is not spoken
who are they crying for today?
I watch the cement dry
the roughness of the aggregate
my sister and I leave the parade
saying your name over and over

Fadwa
the sacrificed
did not cry for martyrs

The mourners arrive
asking for the name of the deceased
my brother and I laugh at these women
who never knew
your morning coffees
nor your side profile
ancestral
the summer dawns
       we loved them too
and the body?
it must be tied to the sun
trace the foliage of the poplars
and leave there bursts of laughter

Black is hard for me to wear
so
against the grain
I made myself beautiful for you
my eyelids are the colours of the sea

This is how we archive the earth
my mother is constellating
without fading
without looking back

back turned to the sun
I will hold on for a long time

You are sitting in the wind
with the coarse thistles
my uncles
and Palestinian chamomile for company
it is the right of the ground

> I, woman, look into the distance
> that is how I say no

I am not allowed jewellery
nor your red scarf and its snowy lacework
what do they know about love Mama?
Your marriage is what we are celebrating
the absurd regained
and time unspent
new earth
remnants of bliss

I do not want fake silences, I want to drift
                              between two birds

I do not put back the veil that falls on my
shoulders
there is nothing to hide

    anyone ever thought of sealing the sky?

I am daughter to the daughter
it falls to me to console
to me to carry   flowers
                                   horizons
my finger points to the first clouds
let us to go home Téta
we will come back tomorrow
pregnant with a new day

I sit facing the void
and call upon all myths of the Orient
it is night time, starless
Téta is howling at the moon
Fadwa, Fadwa
the words find their way to me
imprecise
it is night-time from dream to dream
your dress is flapping on the washing line

like a one last smile in our direction

I keep watch with the wind like two old friends
I am no longer sure I recall
your hands
old in absence

why bother holding on to flesh?

I have a few words for priming
dates
sewing thread
rose water
your winter coat

I will talk about you
all will remember
even the abandoned child

We are at the midway point
of intuition
I start acclimatising
making my way back to the womb of the world

beyond life
beyond evil
we call upon the invisible one
to drink coffee
to break bread

over your armchair, the sun revels
in your amber scents
permanent
fragile

we are filled with secrets

This is why I took a while
we did not have the luxury of seeing eye to eye
we were both
daughter mother
mother daughter
precious
sisters of awkwardness
tied to mess
willing to commit the only murder
that of forgetting
this is why I come back
I am asked to write to you
Fadwa sacrificed woman
be beautiful as everyday
cry out

What to call the summit?
the rest of moderation
or the beauty spot on your chin

we are dawdling in rest contemplating the steadfast
sun-woman

between our tears
children go on playing

nothing is therefore lost

Parachuted into the dawns of others
I no longer want to shield
my eyes from the dance
my patient hips
I would like mourning
to reunite
with all pleasures

how much more time?
when will the body see its day?

The absent one always has to say
there is a trace of wind
cover yourself
we are drawing up the formal notice
of continuity
I find myself copying
her voice
her gestures
like a carrier of the old ways
I ask the children of the continent
have you eaten well?
she is the one worrying
in the quarters of my voice

Fadwa never spoke
    swelling silent
    she could not live close to words

the women of my country die before writing

Make me beautiful in your stories, she would have told me
I make you moon and sacred
you, your back leaning against the last fig tree
unshakeable
fill my life's expanse

Habits end up pouring
out themselves

the butcher opens the blinds
three moon-dogs bark
the first men approach the town
and everywhere love is doing its best

it is as simple as that

I get ready to leave the country
I have left the hyacinths and three memories
melancholy splinters
I have given it
my last
word
I have sewn it on its skin
and on its nails I have painted reunion

Farewell childhood sweetness
the white days of sun
sweetness that gave us callous hands
night eyes
powerful hips
there is no reaping summer
no, Mama
this is how the world starts
with your beginnings
in happy remembrances
of your name

I promise
upheaval
and triumph
for you and Téta
I write us
grains of fire
Mothers of Courage

Emné

I tame exile
without your hands that dig
the sky and its crack
spaces of springtime
the empty flowers of your name

Téta
my hair has grown
do you remember the last river
in my coffee grounds
that foretold my departure?
I had to leave according to the law of the wind
the flowers here have unpronounceable names
there is no wild thyme on a morning
nor the cardamom woman in the depths of their throats

there are only non-places
for the uprooted

I am searching for a square of sun to remind me of you

I arrive in the land of exile
plenty of sun plenty of rain
from a crack I glean a reason for my being here
I am weary, this weather, wind
the curving snow
rite of madness
divisible
bitter
what force keeps me here?
      the snow does not belong to me
in a language of separation
I write myself
rite of bliss
I write to myself
wandering
daring
fanatic
uprooted
ultimate defector

I want to capitalise on emotion and prosper

Remember me, both
I get up each morning and try
to remember
the cardamom woman
the sumac sun
Téta's scarves
and her Sunday lentils
the fig tree
only the felled fig tree

the Mediterranean is a fragile memory
is there anything left to save?
I question the countries that have dwelled in me
the cleared-out sea upon a territory's peak
the beaten earth on the Heliopolis plain
the suburb where I started smoking
this country where it is so cold

I live in a house without features
in intimacy, no familiar scents

Above a murky pond
an eye glimpsed on the horizon
eats between the thighs of the night
telling me to dig deeper

I had a garden with many tulips
a rose bush and a lilac plant, of the common kind
I had a mother who used to lift the sky
with her two hands
aunts who rejoiced over the arrival of water
I was at one with the weather and the secrets of clay

why leave when I was carrying the earth
under my fingernails?

I am searching for
a bittersweet poetry
to wear like a wind skin
to accompany a hundred-year-old child
ready to be born

fists clenched I row
parallel to the mother the void
the word dissolved on awakening
the night that has lasted for twelve days
is this a hell?
are we blessed?
on my island
a zebra by the water's edge
remembers
the message from the day before
delivered by the earth
to those who believe yet refuse to pray

over there
on the edge of the highway
we swap the earth for driving
the pond of slender reeds
the common planes
the straight line of poplars
in my memories my father changes
the radio channel
before switching it off

Drowsiness
anything but talking

uninterrupted

I listen to the sea
I cry

I am no disciple of the spoken word
I make do with my father's letters
my son it has been 300 years since my birth
and the fig tree has always been my shadow's companion
you will cut it down
and God will lose his way
on this here branch
where he was perching

I plant
the arrival of the rain
the split veins of the sun
in a landscape bordering madness
one last house and no anchoring myself
flung into a drunken land
into dawn journeys and laziness
towards a moon coveted by men
how do I live
how do I live I cry at the sky
reflowered by cold, by the word
I flee
insolent and lonely
never leaving the attic of childhood
military kisses on my father's hand
my mother's loneliness
her generous stretch marks
from which the sea and its anger could clearly be heard

I wait for the wind
the dance of the fig tree
the inlet of time

An eternity ago
days yet to be born
to be populated with doubts
can we live uninterrupted?
can we tease out the true meaning of the word?
feet tread and plough the earth
as if probing a new season

I listen to the sea and I pray

I live on an island
without duty or permanence
there I run naked like blood
beautiful like the land at Baalbek
abandoned
like a Christian God
my feet discover
autumns that think they are long summers
the taste of the sugar apple swallowed by my mother
patient sand, rich clay
the bride's gowns on hire
the cry of an animal
      the lure of power
I had thirteen houses
today I live on an island
imagined, fleeting
troubled by tin
yesterday objects
still gathered
an imagined and tangible island
I visit the shadows of certain trees
I scaffold arboreous poems
I throw them into the sea and the sea dances in return
the udders of idleness point towards me
I suck down to the dregs
sometimes a word emerges
that almost defines the resting chill wind

It is cold this evening, I have burned all my money
a cardboard sky floats by
blue magnificent blue
on my island
ginormous perched birds are mating
sometimes I dream them up when they are no longer there
to mimic the flight of chance
I spit fire in the language thought-up by morning
and recite half prayers
I forget how to bow
I am up with the dawn
up for the dawn
and wondering towards which sun should I head

If ever balance was lost
I would return to the cluster of the town
the hospital corridor
and the sachets for swallowing
multicoloured
the birds I would have seen
I would return to the winter where all I would do is wander
from man to man
I would forget midway
the beauty spot on my mother's neck
her white hair her black hair
the sand the salt
the watermelon seeds
her dry heels

I lay down with the stars
to never break from the yardstick overhead
living uninterrupted
without fear
from the three suns

I write a letter
to the childhood country
the loved parent's scent
the village accent never lost
I walk with a pointed dawn
the look of a wandering dog crossing the highway
open mouths fight the midday siesta
I hear complaints uttered in the way of the women
I see them unconscious
with thickset thighs
and childbearing hips
absent from themselves
alive with misery
I do not want to be like them
village arrival
I give the taxi driver money
avoiding his gaze
I answer his questions without giving my name

I always lie
as my mother taught me

No coming back without a gesture of apology
my mother was born in the country of war
news of the dead was daily litany
tombs sank between two bombs
nameless

today the drought
and the sun defying life
but still no story to tell

Leaving the wandering of sterile fields
this is no desert
it is a dry wind plain
years pass without me
scornful I return
set in my countryside ways
what to do with shame

Sunday morning
my aunt cries out
the water has come
the water has arrived
a miracle thrown at the outcasts
we run with our buckets
cans empty stomachs
we fill to the brim
our hands busy
my hands shameful
they are drunk with gratitude
I do not like poverty
nor rejoicing at water

My father was born in the country of war
where a son's layover was daily litany
for a century long no memory was written
the spoken word reigned alone
it alone tamed time
to Baalbek I return
frail among the sacred verses
that hold the town
arrogant disdainful I teach them nothing
ID number 101
revealing the blood of my tribe
at every checkpoint in town
my identity stamped on my elbow
in my childhood
not a desert but a dry wind plain

I stand beside three failing flowers
a sky dark with leg injuries
stillborn the child of the continent
its tooth decayed its neck stuck out
stillborn the cockatoo and its shadow
the summer rain and its weight in gold
the white word plated
the lead placed on God
stillborn the heritage of the hollow fig tree trunk
what a marvel

I drink the world's mess
and fornicate on the heavenly table
at the foot of the parental bed
the wind sleeps with the wind
every morning I feel its bliss

I cough my memory
laugh mad cold
am I going to die tied to madness?
the real finds me
pale and slow
like a lock on a badly covered neck
letting the wind slide the length of the back
in a chasm, God toppled
I am not ill I see everything
the still image of secretion on my fingers
I capture it with a word
everything rings of austerity
I want to go back to the wind bedroom
      I want to awaken it

blind drunk the awakening of the cotton plants the wheat
the inquirer of free will
drunken sun of Magog
dead the roaming of the wolverines

I have set fire to three years
sank my heritage like the slaying of man
in the Mediterranean
I stitched a dream to tomorrow
so that in the daytime a common scent will come

we are nearing the end
man is free to withdraw from a poem
woman free to desert her ancestors' land
blind drunk
I have completed my winters
stillborn
I have no papers left

My anxiety, you know it
it has a tangible form and its own taste
my fear you have fed
deep in the throat
with whitepaper practices
the name badly pronounced
refused entry
I put my destiny between your shoulders
make me a fruitful person
make me a reconciled poet
I am right before your eyes
ready to welcome the news
I am waiting

At what point are you planning to come back?
My only choice is to do as you did

I fled just like you fled
like you I abandoned the mother
and sated all that violence
I had no reason
to deny the word
even if everything pointed to leaving

what would we have done if
        my father
and if
what would I have done

Stirring in the small of my back an epic poem
I am not quick-footed
the bones of fertile women
like my grandmother and her thirteen births
my hips
have been stripped of the lullabies
I wrote, narrated
then made rot
in the coffins of the north
is there a paradise that comes before the body
is there a forgotten book
all stories merge and still today
my child is not born

could it be him who refuses to be birthed?

No matter who was right
I betrayed no-one, neither the mountain
nor the pomegranate trees
I remained she who returns to the depths of the cup
to see appearing
what will come to pass tomorrow
I have not forgotten the signs
the dove
the road
the letter *mim*
Mohamad
the father
carrying a message

I ask the girls of the sky to show me
the next sign

three days in a row a magpie appears at my window
on we go, together
there is room on the contours of my shoulders
secrets for sharing

I will write
despite the predictions
despite the bygone moon

I am an art of open stomachs
yet I have no scream
I have no gesture
I have a name for signing
and a memory to call upon God

If in doubt
always run eastwards
to the place where the birds seek seclusion
to the place where my father was born

if in doubt
do not retell the tale of abandonment
the trees will resent you
even faith will desert you

if in doubt
let the children cradle themselves
there is no freedom in leaving
there are brains for devouring
in the towns that refuse the sun

Sit down all of you under the fig trees
watch their dances
take the time to love
the women who survived

Meet me in Montreal
but do not come without warning
do not come to find my shaved head
the ink, the metal
that I have taken from the winter-women
meet me but do not look at what I have sewn
from freedom to a life of unemployment
in my garden tomato plants
that do not flower
write to me in order to give me some time
I must hide my clothes I must make myself Arabic
in Montreal
place of spiralling
women on the pyre
homes
I look nothing like what you left behind

In this grammar of the world and of injury
I wipe myself from the stomachs of the conquerors
I have signed
Montreal is white
Beirut draws red never-ending
I left in order to come back better
I left my country but I will not sunfade